D0582257

ANIMALS ARE AMAZING

POLAR BEARS

BY VALERIE BODDEN

W
FRANKLIN WATTS
LONDON • SYDNEY

First published in the UK in 2012 by
Franklin Watts
338 Euston Road
London NW1 3BH

Franklin Watts Australia
Level 17/207 Kent Street
Sydney NSW 2000

First published by Creative Education,
an imprint of the Creative Company.

ISBN 978 1 4451 1084 4
Dewey number: 599.7'86

A CIP catalogue record for this book
is available from the British Library.

Printed in China

Franklin Watts is a division of
Hachette Children's Books
an Hachette UK company
www.hachette.co.uk

Book and cover design by The Design Lab
Art direction by Rita Marshall

Photographs by 123RF (Keith Levit), Alamy (Danita Delimont), Corbis (Tim Davis, Steven Kazlowski/Science Faction, Hans Strand, Kennan Ward), Getty Images (Wayne R. Bilenduke, Darrell Gulin, Pal Hermansen, Ralph Lee Hopkins, Norbert Rosing), iStockphoto (Dean Fetterolf)

CONTENTS

What are polar bears?

Polar bears are huge bears. They are the biggest land **predators** in the world! Polar bears live where there is a lot of snow and ice.

A polar bear's fur blends in with the colour of the snow.

predators animals that eat other animals.

Furry polar bears

Polar bears have thick fur. But their fur is not white, it is see-through – like glass! It only looks white because it reflects the white snow and ice. The only part of a polar bear that is not furry is its black nose.

Polar bears have lots of fat under their skin. The fat can be up to 10 centimetres deep. It helps to keep them warm.

Polar bears' fur and fat keep them warm in the cold snow and ice.

Big polar bears

Polar bears are enormous animals. An adult male polar bear can weigh more than 680 kilogrammes. That is more than eight adult people! Female polar bears are smaller than the males. A polar bear standing on its back legs can be three metres tall.

Polar bears stand up to make themselves look even bigger.

Where polar bears live

A polar bear dives off the ice into the Arctic Ocean.

Polar bears live in the **Arctic** in the Northern **Hemisphere** *(HEM-is-feer)*. Polar bears sometimes live on top of ice that covers the **ocean**. They can float for hundreds of kilometres on the ice. Polar bears also live on land. The Arctic has land in Canada, Finland, Greenland, Iceland, Norway, Russia, Sweden and the United States.

Arctic an area at the top of the Earth where no trees grow.
Hemisphere one of the two halves of the Earth. There is one in the north and one in the south.
ocean a big area of deep, salty water.

Polar bear food

This polar bear has caught a seal to eat for dinner!

Polar bears only eat meat. Their favorite food is seals. They use their strong claws and very sharp teeth to catch their **prey**. Sometimes polar bears eat whales or walruses. These animals have **blubber** under their skin. Blubber is good for polar bears to eat.

prey animals that are eaten by other animals.
blubber a special type of fat found inside whales and some other sea creatures that helps keep them warm in cold water.

New polar bears

Polar bear cubs come out of their den in the spring.

Mother polar bears dig a **den** in deep snow. She will give birth to two **cubs** in the den. After about four months, the cubs come out of the den. Their mother looks after them and teaches them to hunt. When the cubs are 2 – 3 years old they leave their mother. Polar bears can live for more than 20 years.

den a home that is hidden, like a cave.
cubs baby bears.

Polar bears swimming

Adult polar bears like to live alone. They spend a lot of their time swimming. They can swim as far as 100 kilometres at a time. Polar bears can swim fast to catch their prey. Their paws are **webbed** to help them move through the water.

A polar bear's head is a long, smooth shape. This helps the bear to swim.

webbed toes that are joined with a piece of skin in between them. Ducks have webbed feet too.

Hunting for food

Polar bears spend a lot of time hunting. They have very sensitive noses and can smell a seal through two metres of thick ice. To catch seals, polar bears sit by holes in the ice. They wait for the seals to come to the holes for air. Then they grab the seals with their strong claws and teeth.

Polar bears keep very still when they are hunting.

Polar bears and people

Today, some people go to see polar bears in the wild. Other people watch polar bears at zoos. Sometimes they can see the polar bears swimming underwater. It is important to learn about polar bears to help protect them in the wild. It is also exciting to see these big bears up close!

Polar bears are popular animals in many zoos.

A polar bear story

Why do polar bears have short tails? The **Native Americans** tell a story about this. They say that a polar bear wanted to know how to catch fish in an icy lake. A fox told the polar bear to put his tail through a hole in the ice. The polar bear did. When he tried to pull his tail out, it was frozen in the ice. His tail was torn off. From then on, polar bears had short tails!

Native Americans the first people to live in America.

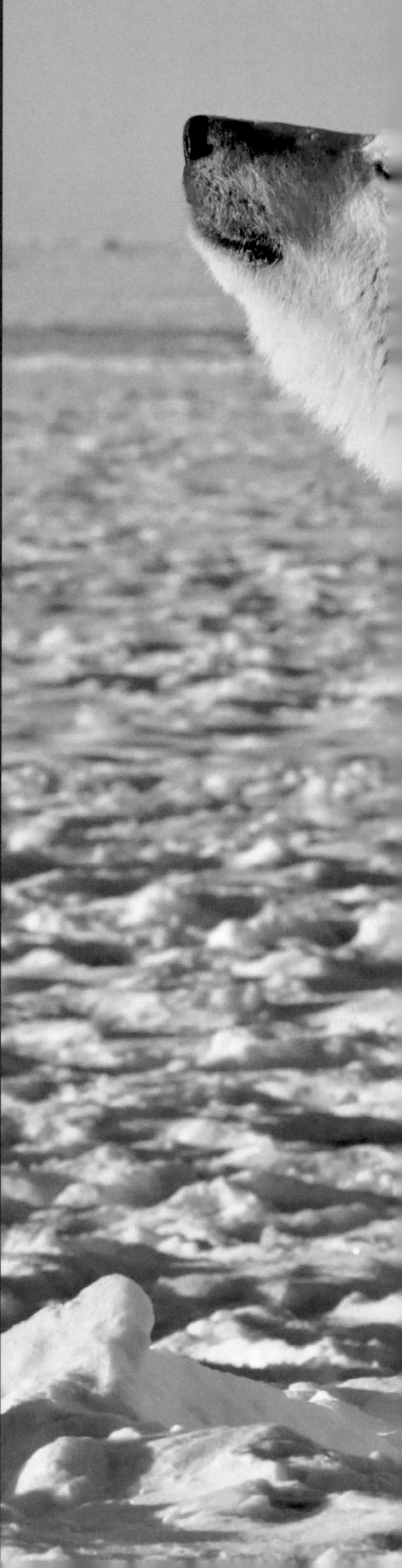